Guido Wandrey

Written, drawn and stuck together by

(Write your name here.)

(Stick your photo here.)

QUEENSGATE

I am a

boy ☐

girl ☐

My name:

My birthday:

Put a cross (X) on your star sign.

I am _____ years old.

Draw candles on
the cake to show
how old you are.

I am already this tall:

_____ cm

My baby teeth:

Put a cross (X) over each tooth that you have lost.

top

bottom

Do you wear braces?

Yes ☐   No ☐

I weigh ___ kg.

My nose looks like this.
Mark one with
a cross (X).

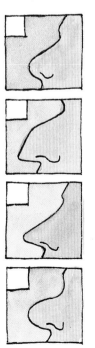

My handprint or footprint:

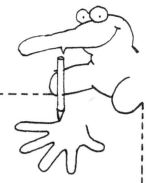

Date: _____

Glasses? Yes ☐ No ☐

Draw some glasses and
freckles on
this face.

My hair colour is _____.

The colour
of my eyes

A lock
of my hair

My hairstyle. Mark one (X) or draw your own.

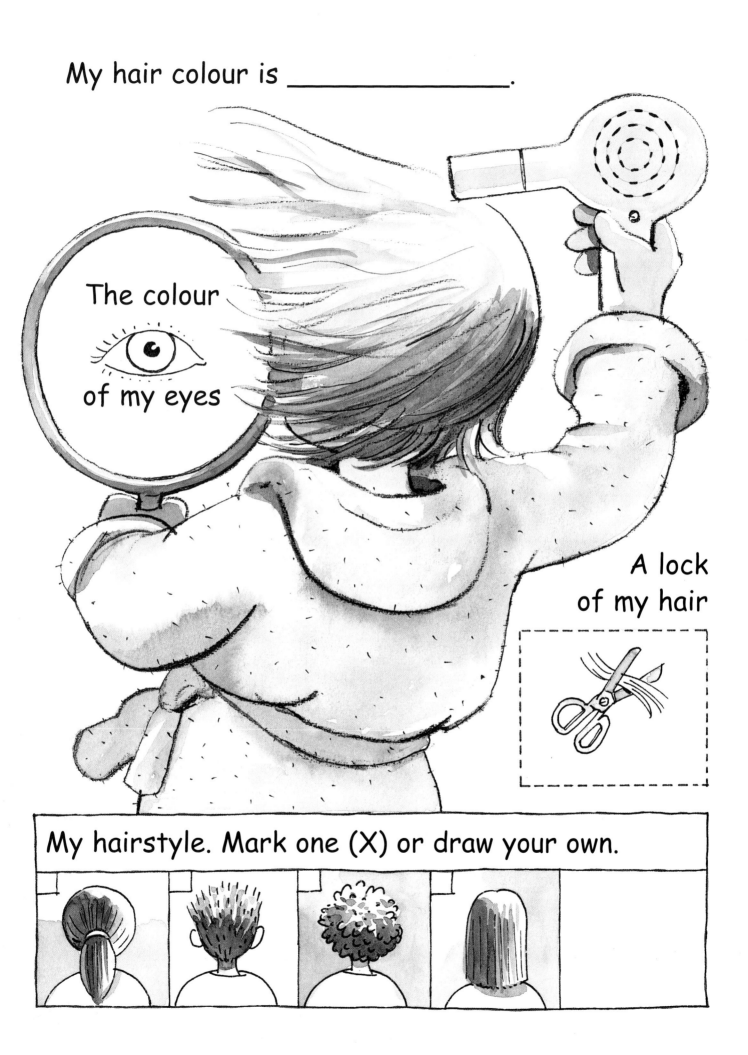

My address:

_____

_____

_____

This is where I live

My country:

_____

I live in . . .

Our house . . .

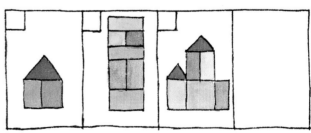

has _____ floors.

A garden ❑   A balcony ❑

What can you see from your windows?

Draw lines between the house and the pictures that show where you live.

My telephone number:

_____

I talk on the phone to:

_____.

Can any of these things be found in your room? Colour in the ones that you have.

Draw pictures of some other things in your room.

Do I have a room all to myself?

Yes ❑   No ❑

I share my room with

_____.

My Family

Who belongs in my family?

_____

_____

_____

_____

_____

_____

My favourite family
photograph

I have brothers and sisters.   Yes ☐   No ☐

How many?

Name and age:

_____

_____

I would like a baby brother or sister.

   Yes ☐   No ☐

My friends and I

Draw a picture or stick in a
photograph of you and your mates.

Their names are:

What we like to do most:

My best friend is _____.

Stick in a
photo of
him or her.

He/She lives:

_____

_____

_____

☏ _____

Sport and Hobbies

I like sport. ❑

I jump. ❑
I run. ❑
I swim. ❑

I cycle. ❑

I play football. ❑
I play basketball. ❑

My favourite sport:

_____

_____

My hobbies are:

_____

_____

I like to draw. ❑
I like to
make things. ❑

Draw a pirate's flag.

These are things I like to play:

_____

_____

_____

My Toys

What will happen in your play?
Draw more characters.

Do you have a puppet theatre?

Yes ☐   No ☐

I have a cuddly toy.

Yes ❑　　　No ❑

Its name is _____.

My favourite toys:

_____

_____

_____

_____

Other toys I would like to have: _____

_____

_____

My Favourite Animal

Mark it with a cross (X).

Is it not there?

My favourite animal is a _____.

My favourite
animal
photograph

My favourite animal has. . .

. . . or draw it yourself.

Do I have a pet?

Yes, I have a

_____.

No, but I would like a

_____.

Its name is _____.

I like to wear this:

_____

_____

_____

My favourite colour is _____.

Colour in the shirt.

My favourite
drink is

_____

_____.

Draw your favourite meal.

Do I play an instrument?

Yes ☐   No ☐

Do I like to sing?

Yes ☐   No ☐

Songs that I like:

_____

_____

_____

_____

My favourite instrument:

What I like to listen to:

_____

_____

_____

I usually listen to:

I find books   fun ☐
interesting ☐
exciting ☐

_____

Books
that I have:

_____

_____

_____

My favourite book:

_____

Draw pictures of your heroes from books and films
or cut out photos and stick them in to make a collage.

What I watch on television:

_____

My favourite programme:_____

My best trip was to

_____.

What did I take with me?
Put a cross (X) on each
to show what you took.

I travelled by...

My funniest
holiday photograph

I would also like to visit _____.

My Day

I get up at ___ o'clock.

What I eat for breakfast:

_____

_____

What I eat for lunch:

_____

_____

I go to school.　　❑

I go to play group.　❑

Lunch is at _____ o'clock.

How I help around the house:

_____

_____

What I do in the afternoon:

_____

_____

_____

_____

Dinner is at ___ o'clock.

After dinner . . .

I read. ❑   I play some more. ❑

Sometimes I am allowed to
watch television. ❑

I go to bed at ___ o'clock.

Through the Seasons

Spring

Which don't fit?

Which don't fit?

Summer

Collect some leaves.
Press them and stick
them in here.

Some pictures are in the
wrong season.

Which don't fit?

Autumn

Which don't fit?

Winter

My favourite season is

_____.

Festivals that I celebrate

Put a cross (X) on the ones you celebrate. Draw the others.

We also celebrate:

_____

_____

_____

My best party

Stick in a photograph.

Decorate these Easter eggs.

List gifts you like to give and receive.

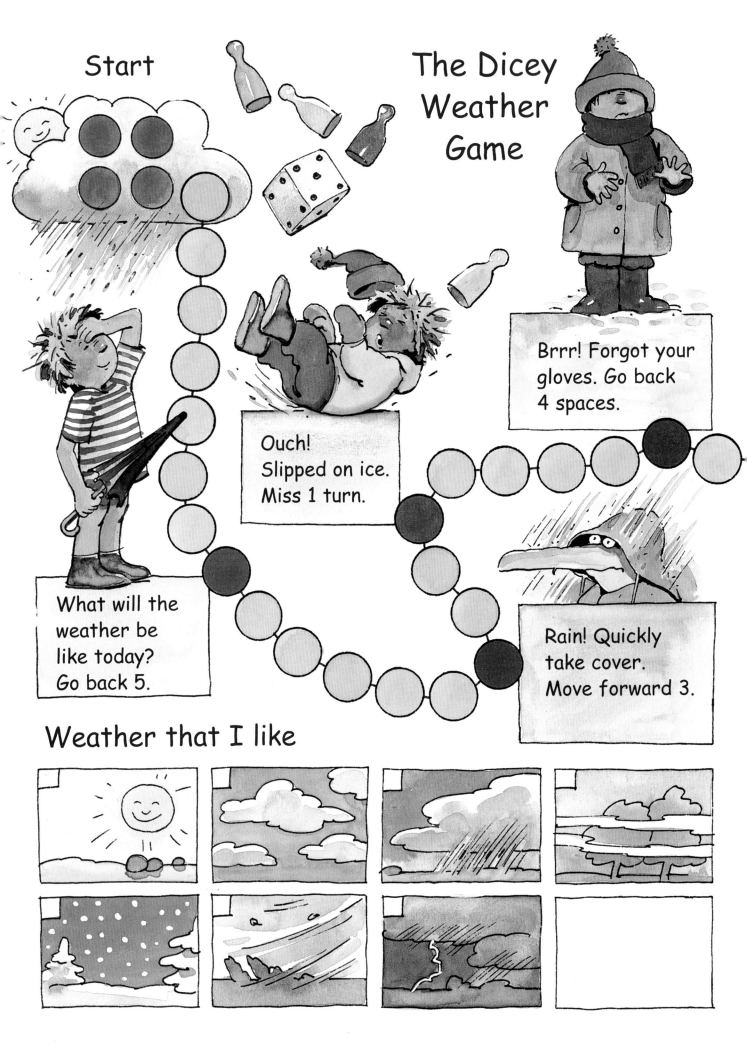

Start

The Dicey Weather Game

Brrr! Forgot your gloves. Go back 4 spaces.

Ouch! Slipped on ice. Miss 1 turn.

What will the weather be like today? Go back 5.

Rain! Quickly take cover. Move forward 3.

Weather that I like

How to play

Each player chooses a counter. Take it in turns to throw the dice and move your counter that number of spaces. When you land on a red hot spot, then you must do as the directions say. The first player to sit in the comfortable chair wins. To reach the chair you must throw the exact number needed to land on the last red space. Keep throwing the dice until you get the right number.

Fog! Go slowly and carefully. Go back 2.

Sunshine! Too hot to move. Miss 2 turns.

Yuck! Wet feet! Miss 1 turn.

A storm! Hurry inside! Move forward 3.

My Best Picture

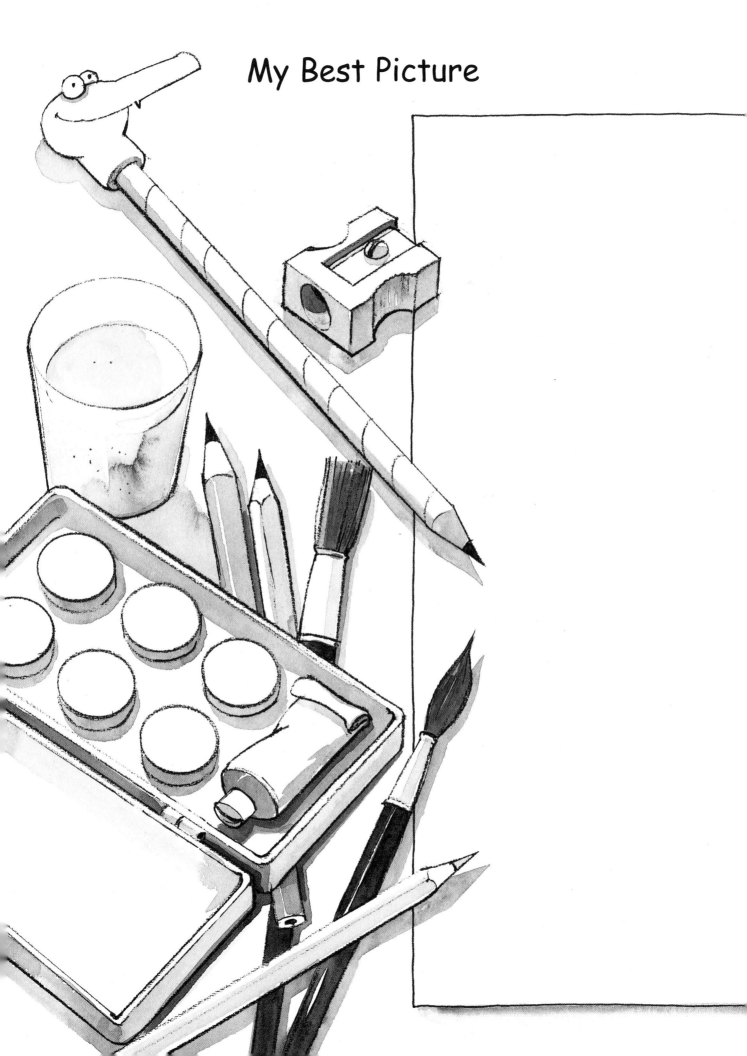

Here is a big space for your very own work of art.

Stick in your best picture or draw a new one.

When I grow up, I want to be:

Write your secret on a slip of paper
and put it inside an envelope.
Seal the envelope and stick it here.

I have done really well with this book, haven't I?

Completed on:

_____Day

_____Month

_____Year